by Pearl Markovics

Consultant:
Beth Gambro
Reading Specialist
Yorkville, Illinois

Contents

PUBLISHING

New York, New York

Hill to Quill

I see a big **hill**.

I see a hot **grill**.

I see a red **drill**.

I see a green **bill**.

I see a small **spill**.

I see a shark's **gill**.

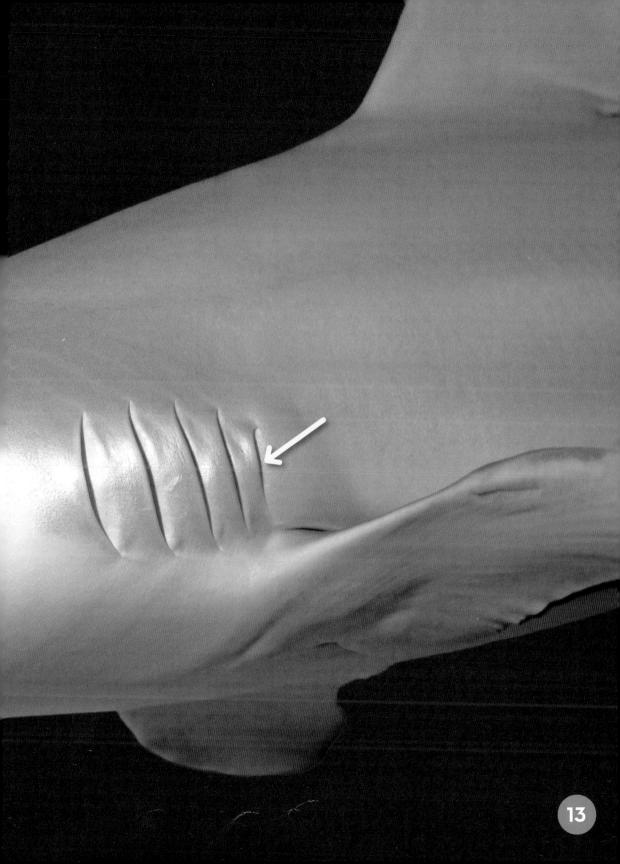

I see a
brown **quill**.

Key Words in the -ill Family

bill   drill   gill   grill

hill   quill   spill

Other -ill Words: **chill, fill, ill, pill**

Index

About the Author

Pearl Markovics enjoys having fun with words. She especially likes witty wordplay.

Teaching Tips

Before Reading

✔ Introduce rhyming words and the **–ill** word family to readers.

✔ Guide readers on a "picture walk" through the text by asking them to name the things shown.

✔ Discuss book structure by showing children where text will appear consistently on pages. Highlight the supportive pattern of the book.

During Reading

✔ Encourage readers to "read with your finger" and point to each word as it is read. Stop periodically to ask children to point to a specific word in the text.

✔ Reading strategies: When encountering unknown words, prompt readers with encouraging cues such as:
   - **Does that word look like a word you already know?**
   - **Does it rhyme with another word you have already read?**

After Reading

✔ Write the key words on index cards.
   - **Have readers match them to pictures in the book.**

✔ Ask readers to identify their favorite page in the book. Have them read that page aloud.

✔ Choose an **–ill** word. Ask children to pick a word that rhymes with it.

✔ Ask children to create their own rhymes using **–ill** words. Encourage them to use the same pattern found in the book.

Credits: Cover, © VDB Photos/Shutterstock, © JethroT/Shutterstock, and © teekayu/Shutterstock; 2–3, © Helivideo/iStock; 4–5, © Alexander Raths/Shutterstock; 6–7, © Rugged Studio/Shutterstock; 8–9, © malerapaso/iStock; 10–11, © SERASOOT/Shutterstock; 12–13, © Nantawat Chotsuwan/Shutterstock; 14–15, © teekayu/Shutterstock and © Marietjie/Shutterstock; 16T (L to R), © malerapaso/iStock, © Rugged Studio/Shutterstock, © Nantawat Chotsuwan/Shutterstock, and © Alexander Raths/Shutterstock; 16B (L to R), © Helivideo/iStock, © Eric Isselee/Shutterstock, and © SERASOOT/Shutterstock.

Publisher: Kenn Goin   **Senior Editor**: Joyce Tavolacci   **Creative Director**: Spencer Brinker

Library of Congress Cataloging-in-Publication Data: Names: Markovics, Pearl, author. | Gambro, Beth, consultant. Title: Hill to quill / by Pearl Markovics ; consultant: Beth Gambro, Reading Specialist, Yorkville, Illinois. Description: New York, New York : Bearport Publishing, [2020] | Series: Read and rhyme: Level 1 | Includes index. Identifiers: LCCN 2019007356 (print) | LCCN 2019012641 (ebook) | ISBN 9781642805987 (ebook) | ISBN 9781642805444 (library) | ISBN 9781642807042 (pbk.) Subjects: LCSH: Readers (Primary) Classification: LCC PE1119 (ebook) | LCC PE1119 .M2854 2020 (print) | DDC 428.6/2—dc23 LC record available at https://lccn.loc.gov/2019007356